PRECIOUS LITTLE GEMS

Ruby Kennedy

ARTHUR H. STOCKWELL LTD.
Torrs Park Ilfracombe Devon
Established 1898
www.ahstockwell.co.uk

First published in Great Britain, 2007

British Library Cataloguing-in-Publication Data.
A catalogue record for this book is available from the British Library.

With many thanks to my friend and neighbour, Mrs Joyce Range, and my sister, Mrs Georgina Hunt, for their encouragement and enthusiasm.

Also, for friendship and practical help from Mr and Mrs J. Miller; and, for believing in my poems, thanks to the publisher, Arthur H. Stockwell Ltd.

Illustrations reproduced by permission of the artist, Mrs E. Ridger.

Part of the royalties from this book will be donated to Cancer Research.

ISBN 978-0-7223-3795-0
Printed in Great Britain by
Arthur H. Stockwell Ltd.
Torrs Park Ilfracombe
Devon

Contents

Jezebel

Sweet that thou art, but also treacherous.
Two potions mixed by a witch long ago.

Poured down thy rosy red lips whilst a baby;
None was about; how could anyone know?

Eyes open wide with the guile of innocence;
Lips dripped with honey; the words that you speak.

Skin white as snow, like the best alabaster;
Jet black the flowing locks on forehead peak.

I loved you once, passionately, ferociously;
Laid bare my soul to the art of your smile.

Thou played with my heart as a siren – precariously
Speaking the honeyed endearments the while.

Now I am left with my life torn in pieces;
Thoughts full of dreams that will never come true.

Whilst thou spins a web ever wide, never ceasing
Catching poor fools, so enamoured of you.

Uncle

We sat at tea,
Old Uncle and me
On a sunny afternoon.
His eyes were as grey
As a winter's sea,
For his time was coming soon.

He talked of a horse he used to ride,
The finest ever seen,
In the army of King George IV
And Mary, his lovely queen.

He said the officer in command
Had entered them for a race,
For the horse, he'd heard,
Was of thoroughbred birth,
And had an excellent pace.

"My old sergeant," Uncle said, with a wink,
"Had thought of a cunning plan.
We'd go round the course the night before;
He'd decide where to make his stand.

"Well, my old horse was like a pal,
Knew every word I said,
And I whispered to him
As I rubbed him down,
And made sure he was watered and fed.

"The day shone bright
As we stood at the start,
With our mates all standing by.
I breathed a prayer to Him up there,
Who rides the eternal sky.

"The flag went down and away we went,
But I kept my horse in check,
'Hold on, old boy,' I said in his ear,
'It isn't our time yet.'

"Some of the lads were yelling,
'Come on, Ernie, try,'
But I held him back
Till I got to the spot
Where the sergeant stood hard by.

"And then I yelled, 'Now show 'em, my love,'
And I let the reins go free.
That horse of mine knew what to do,
He was like a part of me.

"His muscles flexed and his sinews stretched,
And he held his head out high.
With beautiful grace, he took the pace,
And passed the others by.

"I'll never forget that wonderful day;
The cheering came from the heart.
We had the trophy and extra pay;
The horse a new blanket, so smart.

"You know," said Uncle, "I think I'll go
And find that old horse of mine,
And go for a ride." "And I'll come too,"
Said I with a wink so fine.

But then he sat down with a worried frown,
As his poor old legs gave way.
"We'd better leave it this time, girl.
I don't think I could catch him today."

We sat at tea, Old Uncle and me,
Remembering the days gone by.
He knew he'd never ride again,
But he'd love to have a try.

Mischief

Like a ghost in the morning the wind is
Playing games with my bedroom door –
First a glimmer of light round the edges,
And then two inches more.

Click! Whoosh! Bang!
Like a spirit;
Then I suddenly pad across the floor,
Fastening the catch more securely,
And the mischievous ghost is no more.

The Breeze

The breeze rippled the trees,
The stream went hurrying by,
The clouds hung soft in the sky
When I first met you.

You held me in your arms,
We kissed so tenderly,
You vowed your love for me
When I first met you.

How long could this go on?
I thought it could not be;
But our love was so strong
You stayed faithful to me.

When we've grown old and grey,
And life goes hurrying by,
I'd still remember the day
When I first met you.

Our hearts bursting with joy,
That you chose only me;
For ever and for ever
Our lives together will be.

When we've grown old and grey,
And life goes hurrying by,
I still remember the day
When I first met you.

He Is Love

I knew Thee not
'Til I was ill
And my companion, Pain,
Who stabbed me with his fiery sword
So that I cried Thy name.

Long days I lay in misery,
Full of piteous doubt,
And wondered why Thy healing touch
Had seemed to leave me out.

But there was one who watched by me
And tendered every care,
It was my husband, lovingly,
Who nursed me so unselfishly
And restless nights did share.

Good friends came with kindly words,
Bright flowers and pretty things,
Who talked to me so cheerily
Of cabbages and kings.

And was it Thee within the heart
Of husband sweet and true,
And in the hands of Hilda
Who cleaned my house right through,
And in the dear smile of Mary,
Who kept me company,
Who posted letters, made me drinks,
Each day so faithfully?

Yes, it was Thee and now I know
In Love Thou always art.
And my cup really overflows
Because I've seen Thy heart.

Holidays

My friend has gone on holiday –
For six long weeks she's gone away.
I shall not see her every day
To chat about whate'er we may,
While sipping at our coffee.

The air outside no longer rings
With all her children's happenings,
And our small yard is emptying
Of treasures Ann and Sally bring
To show to Auntie Ruby.

My own small lad is lonely too,
He doesn't quite know what to do
To spend each quiet hour through.
No screams, no shouts, no hullabaloo,
No cycle race with David.

We try to bury our spare time
In tiddlywinks and games of mime,
Or making special sweets and cakes
And walking by the parkland lakes,
But who to tell about it?

Although our holidays are fun,
So welcoming the August sun,
And there is plenty to be done,
Yet hurry up and homeward come,
My dearest neighbour, Mary.

To Joyce

It isn't true!
You're seventy?
Well, nobody would know.
Your figure, trim as it can be
And always on the go.
That ever smiling countenance,
So cheerful all the time –
What is the secret sustenance
That helps you toe the line?
At table tennis, softball, tap,
Yes, even rock and roll,
We none of us could overlap
Such an energetic soul.
And when the twinkling feet are still,
The hands come into play,
Knitting lots of lovely garments,
To while the night away.
And painting lovely pictures,
Your forte seems to be;
I bet it gives you lots of joy,
And makes for harmony.

But you know, dear Joyce,
You should be calming down,
And hobbling in your dotage,
With a slightly worried frown.
Instead of playing softball,
Tap-dancing and the like,
You should be going shopping,
On a steady three-wheeled bike.
And in the cosy evenings,
With your knitting in your hand,
A rocking chair would be the thing –
Now doesn't that sound grand?

A Sunny Day

The sun shone through the window,
It shone right on my face.
It made me think of Italy –
That lovely, lovely place.

It made me dream of beaches,
So clean and warm the sand;
Those clear and balmy waters
To float in, getting tanned.

I held my face up to the sun
And thought I heard a song;
A dark and handsome gondolier
Propelling me along.

The great canals of Venice
Beneath the Bridge of Sighs,
Where pigeons in St Mark's great square
Were filling up the skies.

And somehow sitting in my flat
With stitches in my knee,
I felt just like a millionaire –
The sun had shone on me.

Cry for Peace

All that we want is a world full of peace,
Wishing that killing and hating would cease.
Leaders of nations, won't you heed our plea
To stop the cruel slaughter of humanity?

Take all the money that you spend on arms,
Put it to hospitals, houses and farms.
Research a way to make Earth clean again,
Fit as God's Kingdom for women and men.

Mothers who care for their children so long,
Watching each day so that nothing goes wrong;
Feel their hearts breaking, as ever once more
They see their offspring go marching to war.

All of our youngsters think that you don't care,
Seeing the rubbish you put in the air.
Knowing that over each life hangs a threat
Of nuclear warfare; their fate to be met.

We are the keepers of this precious place,
For animals, birds and the whole human race.
Surely you're blind if you just cannot see
What power and greed do to all creatures free.

May Time

The deer a-skipping in the park,
The soaring love song of the lark
That shows that new life has begun –
When April comes, it's May time.

The rabbits pricking up their ears,
The hedgeman clipping with his shears,
Small children feeding ducks with crumbs –
When April comes, it's May time.

Some sparrows nesting in the eaves,
Sweet primroses on grassy leas,
The contented hum of busy bees –
When April comes, it's May time.

One day shower of cooling rain,
Next the sun shines warm again.
All is love, and joy, and fun,
When May time comes.

My Friend

Mary bought me a book,
Yes, Mary bought me a book.
Isn't it really wonderful?
Dear Mary bought me a book.

"Well," you might say to me, "look,
What's so special about a book?"
Mary has three children,
She's a dedicated economist.
She makes her children's dresses
And also makes her own.
She knits her husband's sweaters,
And grows veg for their home.
She's saving hard to buy a house –
At least, that's what she's planned.
So if Mary bought me a book,
It's really rather grand.

It's a book all about Christ and pain
And how through suffering we gain.
And I shall treasure it mightily
Because dear Mary gave it to me.
Yes, Mary gave me a book.

Blackie

When I come home from work
Atop the stairs he grins at me,
Or when I sing a certain song
He howls in harmony.

And with those brown and liquid eyes
He speaks in his own way
To tell of all a dog desires
Of water, food or play.

When Blackie wants some loving
He just climbs up on my lap.
He's thirteen now, and getting on,
But he's not very fat.

For every morn and afternoon,
In rain or cheering sun,
We both go rambling through the woods
To keep us fit and young.

Then Blackie leaps and Blackie trots
And sniffs with boundless joy
At every sweet ecstatic smell
His senses to employ.

He chases all the lady dogs
And gives a cautious growl
At any large and menacing
Opponents on the prowl.

When we are in our home again,
All warmly satisfied,
He stretches out and has a snooze
By our bright fireside.

'Twas Yesterday

'Twas yesterday I met him,
It seems so long ago.
He said I was the sweetest girl
That he did ever know.

And as we walked together
Through wood and leafy lane,
He asked me to be true to him
Till he returned again.

He was a roving gypsy,
As handsome as can be,
Yet in so short a while
I found him all the world to me.

But now my love has gone from me,
There's naught that I can say.
I must have known him always
But 'twas only yesterday.

Tomorrow will be winter,
For me the spring has gone.
The birds may still be singing
But I won't hear their song.

The sun may still be shining
But for me the skies are grey.
I must have known him always
But 'twas only yesterday.

The Secret

Two dear friends, as happy as can be,
Content with each other's company,
Listening to the birds in the treetops fair,
Letting the breeze blow through their hair.

They'd played together when they were small;
Then married two brothers, handsome and tall.
Always there with a helping hand,
Knowing the other would understand
When times were hard, or when life seemed low,
Or rejoicing to watch their children grow.
But in one's heart was a closed door –
A secret she never had told before.

"Oh, Jane, dear, Jane, I need to tell,"
And from her eyes big teardrops fell.
"Cos though I dearly loved my John,
It was your sweet Charles I doted on."

Never a word or deed was said,
Although my heart was torn to shreds.
"Oh, Barbara, dear, don't fret or cry
For your John was the apple of my eye.
But Charles was so good and kind and sweet,
I couldn't deceive my dear helpmeet.
Now they're both gone, we must stay true
To memories of the love we knew."

They hugged each other, and then walked on,
Each with their own thoughts of Charles and John.

Easter Is Coming

Easter is coming, I know that it's true,
For the shy little snowdrops have come peeping through;
The breeze as it blows makes them nod their wise heads
As the bright coloured croci emerge from their beds.

Easter is coming, the birds seem to say
As they swing on the nut cage we fill every day.
The sparrows and blue tits are trilling their best
To choose them a partner and build a new nest.

The soft pussy willow, on bare branches stay,
Turning cotton wool bright from the silvery grey.
Young tender leaf buds begin to unfurl,
As flamboyant cherries show off their pink curls.

The buds on the daffodils wait for the sun
To bring out their gold trumpets now spring has begun.
Yes, Easter is coming, I know that is true,
With a grand simple message for me and for you.

Song of Summer

There is always something sent to make us smile;
Take a look around, you're sure to find it in a while.
Pine trees looking like a waterfall in June,
Honeysuckle scents the summer air,
Birds in the swaying treetops sing a happy tune –
Beauty all around us everywhere.
They're all different; they're all beautiful;
They belong to you and me.

Pansies holding up their faces to the sun,
Daisies in the grass beneath our feet,
Feeding ducks or squirrels is a whole lot of fun –
That's all you need to make a day complete.
They're all different; they're all beautiful;
They belong to you and me.

Watch the magic clouds as they go floating 'cross the sky,
Pink and white, and fleecy as can be,
Islands set in Paradise away up high –
Feasts of joy for hungry eyes to see.
They're all different; they're all beautiful;
They belong to you and me.

Teenager

Is this my child?
This one who looks at me,
With black cold stare,
As if we strangers be.
With lofty thoughts
And supercilious gaze,
Has he forgotten those sweet childhood days?

Is this my child
Who sneers at all I say
And has no time to visit me today?
When there was time;
When all my time was full
Of all his doings,
In or out of school;
When he would sit,
So quiet on my knee
While I was singing
Some sweet melody.

London Not Seen

I've always lived near London,
And yet I knew it not.
I once walked by the Serpentine
When it was very hot.
I marvelled at the many birds
Of varicoloured hues,
All sailing on the water
Or pecking round my shoes.

I once walked through Trafalgar Square
And fed the friendly pigeons there.
Awhile I worked in Wardour Street,
A filing clerk, no less,
I learnt to type contracts for films;
It was a time of stress.

There closeted so close I was
Within the office walls,
I didn't have a chance to see
The real old town at all.
I'd catch a glimpse of Oxford Street
Between work and the Tube,
And little bits of Soho,
Which all seemed rather rude.

I once went to the art gallery
With my two lovely sons.
We stood and gazed for hours
At marvels men had done.
I once went to a minstrel show.
And once a film to see;
Quite recently *Ipi Tombi*
Gave boundless joy to me.
I love the look of old St Paul's;
The stately Sir Big Ben;
If only I'd seen London more
What glorious words I'd pen.

Sally and Ann

Sally and Ann once began to count a string of beads.
Sally went left and Ann went right, to see where it would lead.
Sally came out to a roundabout, Ann sat on a star.
Who'd have thought a string of beads could take you half so far!

Georgina

What has happened to her?
This chirpy little ordinary girl.
Usually the prop round which her household stands
She's got the family in a proper whirl.

Pale and wan and thin.
She droops around the house like some small ghost.
She can't go out, she isn't happy in,
She won't eat even one small piece of toast.

All her children love her –
Rallying around as best they can.
Quietly each morning they get washed and dressed,
Helped by Dad, or coaxed along by Nan.

Why is she in such pain?
Distress and turmoil or that usually happy face.
It's just the seventh time they've moved again –
Her roots are still attached to that last place.

Trees

I really love the trees when they're trembling in the breeze,
Or a strong wind comes to move them all about.
They remind me of the seas, as the waves come in to tease,
Dragging coloured shingle in and out.
So when I feel ill at ease and my routine fails to please,
Or my family and I have fallen out,
I just sit and watch the trees, with their lovely dappled leaves,
And my foolish problems are all put to rout.

Jack the Sailor

Jack the Sailor came on leave to visit his best gal.
"Did you get the message in a bottle that I sent, my darling, Sal?
Also the one I stuffed inside the pudding for your ma?
The other I put in a spicy stew, to please your dear papa!
Did you like the parrot that I taught with extra care
To say to you, 'I love you,' and never once to swear?"
"Oh, Jack," said Sal, "your message never floated near our shore,
And Ma choked on the pudding and fell dead upon the floor.
Poor Pa got dreadful stomach cramps that shook his very fibre.
Then he strangled that damn parrot
Which kept screeching out, 'Elijah.'
For many months you were away; I really could not wait,
So I married Pat the Post, who used to hang around our gate.
Now we have a baby boy, whom we both dote upon,
And we named him Jolly Jack,
Because he should have been your son!"

Sea Lane – Spring

Take a walk down Sea Lane, Middleton,
When springtime is in the air.
A little rain, a little sun, and buds are bursting there.
One more week, or maybe two,
Quite suddenly you'll see
Myriads of golden daffodils
All nodding merrily.

Sat in between them, primroses
And stately narcissi,
With frilled and creamy petals,
Greet each wondering passer-by.

Coming from the busy duck pond,
All the way down to the sea,
It's the miracle of springtime –
Such a treat for you and me.

Sea Lane – Summer

Take a walk down Sea Lane, Middleton,
Sweet honeysuckle scents the air.
First came poppies brightly glowing,
Then the rosebuds, pink, uncurling –
Sounds of birdsong everywhere.

Folk all smile and say, "Good morning" –
Friendly, as in days of yore.
Not a hint of worldly scorning –
Warmth and interest, nothing more.

Breathing in the sea air's pungency
And the flowers' fragrance fair –
Who could fail to feel the magic
Of Sea Lane, now summer's there?

Our Sons

Two little boys, one dark, one fair,
Holding my hand or saying a prayer,
Kneeling down by the side of the bed
Or listening while Pooh Bear stories were read.

Two little lads, one tall, one small,
But somehow that didn't matter at all.
In winter when paths had a snow attack
The elder would carry his bro on his back.

The youngest one was accident-prone,
The eldest meandered dreamily home.
Two growing lads with an occasional mood,
Yet neither of them were ever rude.

I loved them both through the teenage years,
They comforted me when I knew tears.
With their father away I looked after them good,
I made some mistakes, but they understood.

Two young men, both handsome and strong,
With responsible jobs, working hard and long.
Living in opposite parts of the land,
Yet always ready to give a hand
To each other, or Mum and Dad –
Our two lovely sons, what a blessing we've had!

Jesus, My Lord

Who sees me through the day,
And hears me when I pray?
Who helps me on my way?
– Jesus, my Lord.

Who knows my every care,
My joys and sorrows share?
Whose love is always there?
– Jesus, my Lord.

There was no hope in me;
I could forever be
Lost in my misery
Without my Lord.

Living a life of sin,
Following Satan's whim,
Selfishly giving in
To my despair.

Then like a star so bright,
He came into my sight.
Who made my darkness light?
– Jesus, my Lord.

He died at Calvary,
Hung on that cruel tree,
From sin to make us free
– Jesus, our Lord.

The Circus – Phase One

At first I was just a lowly groom –
The horses I loved and adored.
To feed and to clean them and make their coats shine
Was a joy and my life it consumed.

But after a long day of horse care,
Plus two shows in which I performed,
I'd go to the back end of the monkey wagon
Where my bed was – alone and forlorn.

Then I started to become an artiste –
It was a spectacular thrill.
I was promised a new place to live in,
But the promise was never fulfilled.

At the end of the day
I still slept there
In that cramped little van,
With the monkeys behind the partition –
That mischievous chattering clan.

Tho' I rode on my governor's best thoroughbred mare
In Tyrolean costume so grand,
The clowns called, "Miss Ruby, what are you doing there?"
As we rumbaed to the strains of the band.

I would take Susan back to her stable,
Rub her down, put her cover around;
Return just as soon as I was able
Or out went the lights 'ore my bed I got down.

Then I'd cry in my little compartment,
The monkeys would chatter and jeer
And steal my clothes through the partition,
So I left at the end of that year.

The Circus – Phase Two

Oh, my life in the circus was wonderful,
Tho' it had its ups and its downs.
Flying on a trapeze was delightful –
I felt great in my short sequinned gowns.

As I rode on a horse round the sawdust ring,
Vaulting upon her back with a yell,
Standing high with small treads,
Hanging down with my head
To pick up some flags, I felt swell.

So my life in the circus was wonderful –
I went on to become quite a star.
Not quite famous, but favourably thought of –
Even travelling to places afar.

The folk in the circus were lovely –
Cameraderie I've never seen since.
The putting up of tents in the wind and the rain,
Performing, then pulling it all down again –
You'd think they'd the life of a prince.

So my life in the circus was exciting –
It had its laughs and tears.
So if I had the chance to do it all again,
I certainly would – never fear.

Love Song

Is this love
When happiness is only when you're near me?
Is this love
When you are much too deep in thought to hear me?
Is this love
When everything I say or do
Depends on just a smile from you,
And everything you do or say
Means you don't even glance my way?

Is this love
When my poor heart is lonely and so hungry?
Is this love
When you distribute love to all and sundry?
Is this love
When every moment we're apart
Means one more piece of a broken heart,
But every moment near to you
Means spring has come and all is new?
And, yes, it's love,
It's really, really love.

Through the Eyes of the Elderly

When I came to this hospital
My mind was not quite right.
I had quite perfect arms and legs
And a healthy appetite.
Yet after only just one year
My arms and legs won't work, I fear.

I'm heaved and herded to and fro
From toilet to table and back I go.
It's "Do sit down, dear Mrs Brown,
In case you have a fall."
It seems, although I want to,
I mustn't walk at all.

I could stand up all by myself
To get out of my chair,
If only they would give me time
To make my way out there.

The nurses have a lot to do,
And of them there are very few.
If only they would understand
We'd like to help whene'er we can.

So, nurses, please, your lives would be
Much easier if you'd just let me
And all the frail and elderly
Use our hands and arms to rise
And strengthen muscles in our thighs.

To feel I belong to myself sometimes
May help my poor bewildered mind,
And lighten perhaps the load you bear,
Because of us for whom you care.

Do We Want War?

The children we have cherished
And protected all their life.
We tried to teach them loving ways
Without the fear of strife.

The older generation,
Who have seen it all before,
Know there is nothing to be gained
By marching off to war.

In days gone by, 'twas glorious
To fight for England's name,
At least so we were told,
And we believed it just the same.

We fought for a just cause,
And we were proud to fly the flag
To show the world we cared
And put a tyrant in the bag.

The war to end all wars, they said,
And we believed that too,
But now it's all begun again –
Unbearable, but true.

What is the answer? Who can tell?
Should we procrastinate
And let the terrorists stockpile
More fuel for their hate?

We don't want war,
For poor and hungry innocents
Will suffer even more.
The world is turned in turmoil –
People frightened, battered, sore.

We have to pray to God above,
More than we've ever done,
That He who understands
Just how it feels to lose a son
Will stop these wars.

Jamie's Friend

Down our street there's a man who makes baskets –
Something that nowadays you very rarely see.
He works all alone, in a hut, on a green,
And doesn't go home 'til it's time for tea.

He's very, very deaf and you have to write the orders
On some pieces of white paper that he keeps handy by.
Although he's very lonely, you never hear him grumble;
He's working much too hard to ever ask the reason why.

I think he's very glad that I go to visit him.
I write him little letters and I watch him with the cane,
Making shopping baskets, cat baskets, dollies' cots and other things;
Wet it, weave it, hammer it and then begin again.

He told me that he's sixty-seven, has ten fine children
And he's very soon retiring to Brighton by the sea.
So he said to tell my mother, "You'd better get your order in
If you want to buy some wickerwork from me."

Tribute to Bob Phipps
(Mullard's Amateur Dramatic Society)

There was a man,
Quite small of stature, yet so grand,
Whose smile so fine
Would make the sun to shine
On children, pets, his family and friends,
Tho' stricken with a fiend that would not mend.

He hadn't much,
Except a kind and loving touch
To all he knew;
And everything he'd do
To help his mates in any way he may,
Tho' fighting with a malady each day.

When he would sing
He'd make the rafters ring,
And his sweet voice
Would make your heart rejoice.
There he would stand,
Eyes closed and gently outstretched hand,
Singing into our lives
Love's ever promised land.

We do not know
Why our friend had to go.
Perhaps the Heavenly Father knew him best,
And thought it time that Robert had a rest.
Oh, we will miss you greatly, Bobby dear.
We'll think about you always, year on year.

Christmas Time Again

It seems it's Christmas time again –
For many, a joy, for others, pain.
Those folk who are all alone at last
May reminisce of Christmas Past,
When they were young, strong and gay
And had such fun on Christmas Day.

Come, cheer up, dears, there's still the tele
To help your Christmas time be merry.

You still can see the children play
With toys that come on Christmas Day.
Those dolls that walk, talk and cry,
And games we couldn't even try.
Sophisticated toys, may be,
Still starry eyes light up with glee.
Santa still cries, "Ho! Ho! Ho!"
While little ones play in the snow.

The Christmas story still runs true,
Sweet bells ring out for me and you.
So for a while forget your pain,
For Christmas time is here again.

To Barry Vines
(Entertainment Officer, Cenae Hill Hospital)

Mornings are so lovely
Now that summer's come at last.
The thrushes hopping through the woods
Can find a rich repast.
All the trees and bushes are full to bursting green,
And pink and white may blossom –
Is a glory to be seen.

Hear the rook caw-cawing
In the highest branch nearby,
And cheers and thrills and whistles
Fall like raindrops from the sky.
A multitude of joyous sound
Above the dappled grass,
All free for us to savour,
Now summer's come at last.

Fallen Destiny

There once was a creature called Man,
Who was part of God's wonderful Plan
To live on the Earth
And to fill its great girth
With the fruitfullest loving clan.

But given this bounteous joy,
Man did nothing but kill and destroy
All the creatures around,
The fresh air and the ground
With pollution. His time to employ.

Soon the treasures will all disappear –
No sweet flowers, no soft running deer.
Will God wake up to see
No more Earth, no more sea,
No more clan,
No more Man,
No more Plan?

Local Artist

7 years a Circus Performer

20 years N.H.S.

Retired to Middleton

1998